Arm Knitting

First edition for the United States published in 2015 by
Barron's Educational Series, Inc.

© RotoVision 2015

All inquiries should be addressed to:
Barron's Educational Series, Inc.
250 Wireless Boulevard
Hauppauge, NY 11788
www.barronseduc.com

Publisher: Mark Searle
Editorial Director: Isheeta Mustafi
Commissioning Editor: Jacqueline Ford
Editor: Erin Chamberlain
Assistant Editor: Tamsin Richardson
Design concept: JC Lanaway
Page layout: Tony Seddon
Step-by-step photography: Peter Weber
Beauty photography: Ivan Jones and Neal Grundy
Cover design: Michelle Rowlandson

Library of Congress Control Number: 2015941220

ISBN: 978-1-4380-0730-4

Printed in China

9 8 7 6 5 4 3 2 1

Arm
Knitting

Amanda Bassetti

BARRON'S

Contents

Projects 50

Introduction

I learned to knit on needles just a couple of years before teaching myself to arm knit.

As a beginner knitter, I had the same issue many other knitters have. I never completed a project because it took such an incredibly long time. I would excitedly start a new project, wanting to wear something that I had made for myself, and then, three or four hours and five or six mess-ups later, I would disappointedly give up. I worked forty hours a week at that time and I just did not have the hours to spend on those extremely long knitting patterns. So I set out on a mission to find a solution. I was determined!

In 2011, I typed "giant knitting" into YouTube™ hoping to find something I could learn to create fast patterns. And I did. However, I needed expensive, large needles and wool that cost over $300 for a blanket. This was not practical for me. I kept scrolling … and I saw it! A woman facing the camera, knitting something very quickly with incredibly thick yarn. I was inspired! I watched for about 20 minutes trying to figure it out step-by-step. It was difficult because she was not teaching; she was just quickly moving her arms and creating an amazing piece of artwork. This was arm knitting. I taught myself and then went on to share it with others. I wanted to teach everyone how to arm knit a scarf in just 30 minutes, with wool that cost less than $10! The response was amazing.

The simple, 10-minute, step-by-step arm knitting video that I uploaded to YouTube™ went viral after just a few weeks. Since then, arm knitting has become my passion. You can see my knitting videos on my blog, *simplymaggie.com*. This book is special to me because it gathers five years of blogging together in one place and gives me the opportunity to teach you new and exciting ways to create your own pieces of art.

On the following pages, you will find 30 different patterns that I created with love and passion, especially for this book. Patterns that are possible for anyone, from beginners to experienced knitters, who just want to whip up a new blanket in less than an hour.

I absolutely love to arm knit! I hope everyone who sees this book is as inspired as I was.

Amanda Bassetti

Decorative Throw (see page 118 for pattern)

Arm Knitting Basics

What Is Arm Knitting?

Arm knitting is the fastest way to learn how to knit and to complete a knitting pattern. Most patterns are completed in under an hour! Now that's fast knitting.

If, like me, you are among the large number of knitters who never seem to have the time or motivation to finish a knitting project, then arm knitting is for you! It is also great for beginner knitters who want an easy yet interesting way to knit a variety of beautiful, chunky-style pieces in a small amount of time.

All you need is a little time, a skein or two of chunky to super-bulky yarn, this handy book, and your arms. That's it! No needles are required for any of these patterns. Arm knitting saves you money and eliminates the confusion of which needles to purchase for each pattern. Sounds simple, right? It really is, once you learn the six basic steps to finishing any arm knitting pattern.

With step-by-step instructions for each stitch and pattern, including photos and tips, you will master the basic—and even the more ambitious—arm knitting patterns in no time at all.

With this technique, you can create pieces ranging from blankets to headbands and everything in between. You can arm knit something for every season, every outfit, and every room in your home. When writing this book, I set out to create never-before-seen arm knitting patterns, and that's exactly what I did. Using the knowledge of which stitch works best with which accessory or home décor item, this book brings you the best patterns available. I will show you how to arm knit seven different stitches, and techniques for increasing and decreasing to create different shapes. I will also show you how to create 30 different projects with a variety of yarn materials and colors to keep your collection of arm knitted pieces exciting.

Under each project in this book, I will share which yarn was used and how many yards you will need to complete the project in total. So if that specific yarn is not available, you can find something similar and be sure you have enough to complete your new project.

Let's get started!

Mega Infinity Scarf (see page 82 for pattern)

Materials

There are three basic things to keep in mind when picking out the yarn for your project:

- Size or weight

- Content or blend (for example, wool, acrylic, or cotton)

- Yardage

Tip

Remember to double or triple the yardage when using multiple strands at the same time.

When you are arm knitting, the size of your stitches depends on the size of your yarn, the size of your wrist, and how tight you keep your stitches.

With most projects, the bulkier the yarn, the better it will look. For example, if you use a basic chunky yarn in category 5 bulky weight/13 ply when you are arm knitting a blanket, you will end up with larger holes. This will make for a not-so-cozy blanket. No one wants to cuddle up with a fishnet. Stick to super bulky or even giant-sized yarn when knitting larger-scale items. It is a good idea to double or triple the number of strands so that you are arm knitting with two or three strands at one time. With most arm knitted pieces, the fuller it is, the better it looks.

When you are arm knitting some smaller-scale items, such as a cowl or a headband, using two strands of bulky yarn will work very well. The holes in between the stitches will be larger since the yarn is not as full, but this will still give you a great looking knitted accessory.

There will be a brand and type of yarn suggested under each pattern. The suggested yarn will give you the best results for that pattern. However, if you cannot purchase that particular yarn, one of similar size and texture will also give you great results. See page 128 for more information on substituting yarns.

If you look on the back of any yarn wrapper it will tell you the weight or size as well as the yardage and contents of its fibers. There are a few weights of yarn that work best with arm knitting patterns.

- Chunky or Bulky, Craft or Rug yarn (category 5 bulky weight/13 ply). This yarn is normally used on size 8–11 (metric size 5–8 mm) knitting needles.

- Super Bulky or Roving yarn (category 6 super bulky weight/14 ply). This yarn is normally used on size 11–17 (metric size 8–12.75 mm) or larger knitting needles.

- Jumbo, Roving, Giant or Big Stitch yarn (category 7 jumbo weight/20 ply). This yarn is normally used on size 17 and larger (metric size 12.75 mm and larger) knitting needles.

The texture of the yarn does not matter as much as the size. You can choose the texture based on your personal preference. For rugs, mats, and home items that endure harder wear, you may want to choose durable wools, such as alpaca yarn, T-shirt yarn, or rope-type yarn. Accessories and blankets can be made with softer yarns. Be sure to save and follow the care instructions on the yarn wrapper if you plan to wash your items.

Yarn Weights

Yarn weight refers to the thickness of the yarn. The weight of the yarn can have a significant impact on your finished project. Choosing a size 5, 6, or 7 weight yarn makes for a fuller end product, rather than one with large holes. If you can't get really thick yarn, you can double or triple your strands for a fuller look, too.

STANDARDIZED YARN WEIGHT	US	UK/EUROPE	AUSTRALIA/NZ
0	Thread Cobweb Lace Light Fingering	1 ply 2 ply 3 ply	1 ply 2 ply 3 ply
1	Fingering Baby	Sock 4 ply	4 ply
2	Sport	Light DK 5 ply	5 ply
3	DK Light Worsted	DK 8 ply	8 ply
4	Worsted Fisherman Aran	Aran 10 ply	10 ply
5	Bulky Rug Craft	Chunky	12 ply
6	Super Bulky Roving Ploar	Super Chunky Polar	14 ply
7	Jumbo Roving	Super Bulky	20 ply

A selection of different weights of yarn.

Getting Started

When starting any arm knitting project, you will need to learn the basic six steps to complete any pattern. You will find these on the next page. But before you start, here are some important things to remember:

- Know which strand is the working yarn and which strand is the tail. The working yarn is the yarn that is being pulled from the center of the skein of yarn. The tail is what you will use, after making a slipknot, to cast on your stitches. Once you have done this, the tail will no longer be used throughout the pattern.

- Keep all of your stitches as tight as you can on your arms. The looser your stitches are, the larger the holes will be in your project. Tightening the first stitch when switching stitches over to the opposite arm can be tricky. Be sure that you understand this step (see pages 24–25) and apply it to each pattern.

- When using multiple strands of yarn at the same time, pull the strands from the center of each skein of yarn. This prevents the skeins from moving around and will avoid a mess of tangled yarn in the middle of a project!

- Completing a project in one sitting is much easier than coming back to it later. Purchase enough yarn ahead of time so that you can start and finish your project without stopping.

- If you need to stop knitting while working on your project, simply knit all of the stitches to one arm, pick up the yarn, and carry it with you. Alternately, you could put all the stitches onto a pipe cleaner until you can return to finish your project.

- You may find if you pull on the tail once you have finished knitting, you may accidentally shorten the cast on edge. To prevent this, knot the tail in the same way that you knotted the tail on the bound off end.

- If a stitch gets snagged during wear, don't worry! Grab each end of your finished project and pull. This forces the stitches to go back to the length they should be.

Keeping all of these tips in mind will help you avoid any frustrating moments when learning how to arm knit.

Circular Mat (see page 92 for pattern)

How to Arm Knit

Here is a summary of the six basic steps you need to learn to complete any arm knitting project:

1. Making a slipknot

This is the first step in any knitting project. Tying the slipknot creates your very first stitch. Once you have completed your slipknot you can begin to cast on, making your project wider and longer as the pattern directs (see page 20 for instructions).

2. Casting on your stitches using the long-tail cast on method

Casting on your stitches with this method will ensure a good-quality edge and start to your project. The last thing you want is an edge that looks uneven and loose. Keep these stitches as tight as you can. The tighter you keep your stitches, the better your project will look (see page 22 for instructions).

3. Arm knitting your stitches

This is the part of the project where you will use different stitches. Arm knitting your stitches creates the "body" or main part of any arm knit project. Again, be sure to keep all of your stitches as tight as possible to keep your project looking its best (see page 24 for instructions).

4. Binding off your stitches

This is how you end the process of arm knitting. When binding off, you will want to keep the stitches loose so that this end of your project is not smaller or skinnier than the cast on edge (see page 26 for instructions).

5. Sewing the ends of your project together

Sewing the ends of your project is only necessary for projects that are circular in shape, for example, an infinity scarf or a cowl. In most projects you will be using the leftover "tail" of yarn from casting on to sew the ends together, or you can cut the tail long enough after binding off and use that to sew the ends. Either way works perfectly (see page 28 for instructions).

6. Weaving in the ends

This is an optional step, but I recommend you do this with every project to be sure it never falls apart. Weave in the ends after creating that last tight knot at the end of your project. Also weave in the tail at the cast on edge (see page 29 for instruction).

Once you have mastered these six very simple steps, you will be able to complete any knitting project. You can also move on to learning new stitches, see pages 32–49.

Make sure you have your materials on hand before commencing your project.

Slipknot

Pull a strand of yarn from the center of the skein. You are now ready to start the very first step to arm knitting any project—making the slipknot. Pulling the yarn from the center of the skein will make arm knitting any project easier, as it will eliminate a mess of tangled yarn from the skeins moving around.

How to make a slipknot

1. Pull the length of tail suggested for the pattern from the center of the skein (or skeins, if you are using more than one) of yarn. If using multiple strands of yarn at the same time, use them as if they are one strand.

2. Drape the yarn over your hand and pinch the strands together below your hand.

3. Twist the loop clockwise and grab the working yarn.

4. Pull the working yarn through to create a new loop and pull tight.

5. Place this loop on your arm.

Casting On

This is how to cast on your stitches using the long-tail cast on method. This method is the most secure and sturdy way to cast on your stitches. Remember—your slipknot counts as your first stitch.

How to cast on

1. With the slipknot on your right arm, put your index finger and thumb between the strands. Hold the working yarn and the tail against the palm of your hand with your ring and pinky fingers.

2. Widen your thumb and index finger, so that the strands make an "X" over your left thumb and finger.

3. Move your right index finger under the strand of yarn that is wrapped around the outside of your left thumb and closest to your left wrist. Then take it over the strand on the inside of your left thumb.

4. Grab the farthest strand that crosses around the front of your left index finger with your right thumb and index finger.

5. Pull that strand up while holding the working yarn and tail with your left hand. This creates a new loop, which is your second stitch.

6. Place this new stitch on your right arm.

7. Cast on the number of stitches that the pattern calls for.

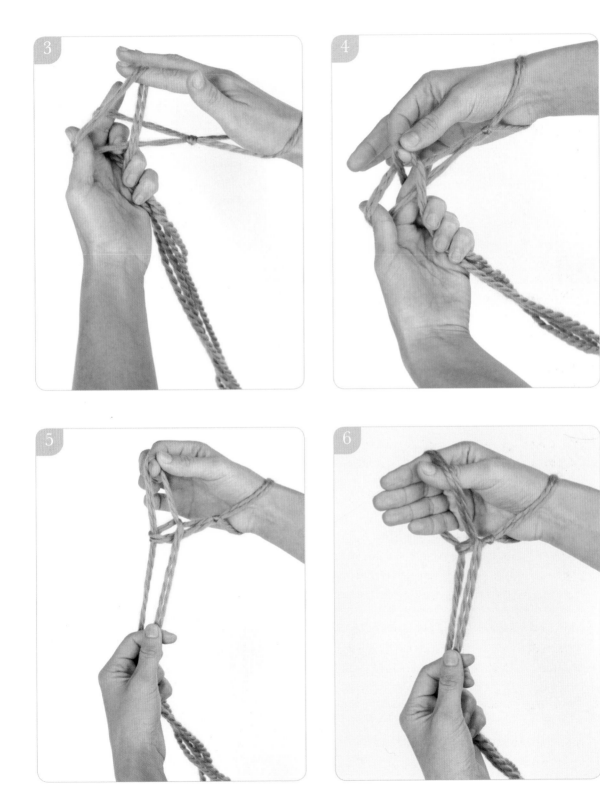

Knitting

This is the process that will create the body or main part of your project. Here you will learn to use the basic "knit stitch," used in every project.

Arm knitting your stitches

After casting on, begin by arm knitting your stitches over to the opposite arm, creating new stitches.

ROW 1

1. Hold the working yarn in the hand of the arm with all of the stitches on it. Pull the first stitch over and off your hand while still holding the working yarn. The working yarn loop creates a new stitch.

2. Turn that stitch toward you and slide it onto your other arm.

3. Tighten that first stitch by pulling the working yarn and pushing up on that "knot" until you can not tighten it anymore.

4. Continue arm knitting all of the stitches over to your other arm by repeating steps 1 and 2, keeping all of the stitches as tight as possible.

ROW 2

5. Hold the working yarn in the hand of the arm with all of the stitches on it. Pull the first stitch over and off your arm creating a new stitch.

6. Turn that stitch toward you and slide it onto your other arm.

Repeating these two rows using knit stitch will create the look of the stockinette stitch on the right side and the garter stitch on the other side (the wrong side).

This is the most basic stitch when arm knitting because the working yarn always stays in the front of your work and you knit every stitch and every row the same way.

The only difference between knit stitch and other stitches is moving the working yarn from the front of your work to the back by picking up the skeins and lifting them up and over your work, placing them in your lap closer to you when the stitch calls for it.

Knit stitch is my favorite to use on blankets and infinity scarves. It is a really fast stitch because there is not a lot of movement other than moving the stitches from arm to arm.

Tips

- You will no longer be working with the tail.
- Remember to keep all of your stitches as tight as possible!
- To tighten the first stitch when moving it to the opposite arm, you will need to pull the working yarn while pushing the knot up toward your arm.

Binding Off

Binding off is the step that will end your project. When you bind off, you have completed arm knitting and will be moving on to the finishing steps that will make your project complete.

How to bind off

1. Knit two stitches to your other arm.

2. Pick up the first stitch that you knitted and lift it over the second stitch and off your arm. Tighten your work up just a little bit. You are left with one stitch on your arm.

3. Knit one stitch.

4. Pick up the first stitch on your arm and lift it over the second stitch and off your arm.

5. Repeat steps 3 and 4 until you have just one stitch left on your arm.

6. Leaving the last stitch on your arm, cut the working yarn approximately 2 feet (60 cm) away from your arm and pull that long tail through the last stitch on your arm to create a knot. Pull the knot tight.

Tip

Don't bind off too tight or the end of your project will not be the same width as the cast on edge. It will be skinnier, creating an odd-shaped knit piece.

Sewing the Ends

Sewing the ends together is not necessary for every arm knitting project. Use this step for projects such as the infinity scarf, cowls, or a pillow. If you are arm knitting a blanket, for example, skip this step and move on to the next one.

How to sew the ends of your project

1. Turn your project inside out and place it on a flat surface so that the wrong side of the stitch is facing you.

2. Fold your project in half so that the two ends meet.

3. Line up the cast on and bind off edge stitches the best you can.

4. Using the leftover ends, or the "tail," sew the ends together by threading the yarn through each stitch from both the cast on and bind off edges. Make sure to go through each stitch on the edge for an even look.

5. On your final stitch, pull the strand halfway through—create a loop—and then pull the tail through that loop, creating a knot.

6. Tighten the knot.

Weaving in the Ends

Weaving in the ends is an extra step that will ensure that your arm knitting project will never fall apart. After making that last knot on the edge you can just cut the tail, but I highly recommend taking an extra minute or so to weave it into the edge of your project. This will ensure that your project will last as long as possible.

How to weave in the ends of your project

1. Turn your project inside out. Take the excess yarn you have from sewing the edges together and making that last knot and weave that through the edge of your scarf a few inches. If it makes it easier for you, you can use a crochet hook to grab the tail and pull it through the edge stitches. Just stick it under the stitches you would like it to go through, wrap the tail around the hook, and pull it through, being careful not to snag a stitch on the edge.

2. Cut the excess yarn an inch (3 cm) from the last stitch you wove it through.

3. Turn your project right side out and admire your beautiful, great-quality seam.

Arm Knitting Stitches

Before You Begin

Arm knitting different stitches will give you the opportunity to create many different chunky-style pieces to wear or use in your home. Not only does the stitch change shape but some stitches look fuller with smaller holes, some stitches will make the project lay flat, while others will create edges that curl. Each stitch has its own look and feel, and you won't regret putting in the extra few minutes to learn each stitch.

If you usually knit with needles, you may notice some differences in the instructions in this chapter on how the stitches are worked from row to row.

One of the biggest differences between knitting with your arms and knitting with needles is that when knitting on needles you turn your work around between every row and knit a "wrong side" and "right side." When you knit using your arms you can't turn your work. Essentially, you are only knitting one side. This means that knitting different stitches will work a little differently when you are arm knitting.

Another difference is that with needles you are able to move the working yarn from the front of your work, and then to the back of your work to purl stitches quite easily. When arm knitting, it is a bit more complicated, but I have come up with a way to make it possible to knit different types of stitches by moving the working yarn back and forth. It does take a little bit longer than the basic knit stitch, but the results are beautiful and the projects can still be completed much faster than if you are using needles.

The trick I have come up with to make it go a little bit quicker, and to prevent the headache of tangled yarn, is to place your yarn in a bag. I like to use a cotton bag to avoid the noisy crinkling of a plastic bag. Then you just simply pick up the bag, lift it over your work and toward you to the back of your work, place it on your lap, and work your next stitch(es) with the yarn in the back.

When learning new stitches, be patient. Some of them took me a while to learn! But once you get it, it is incredibly simple.

Winter Snood (see page 100 for pattern)

Knit Stitch

If you want to get a project done in no time at all use the knit stitch; it is the most basic arm knitting stitch and is used in every item in this book. It is great for beginners to learn quickly and it always looks beautiful, whether used on a simple scarf or giant blanket. You work the yarn in front of your work throughout the entire project, so there isn't much thinking involved. It is a great stitch for arm knitting in front of the TV!

How to use knit stitch

First: Make a slipknot and cast on your stitches (see pages 20–23).

1. Hold the working yarn in the hand of the arm with the stitches on it.
2. Slip the first stitch off your arm and over the working yarn.
3. While still holding the working yarn, turn the stitch toward yourself and slip it onto your other arm. Tighten the first stitch by pushing the "knot" up toward your arm while pulling the working yarn at the same time. All of your other stitches can be tightened by simply pulling on the working yarn.

Repeat these steps with all of the stitches until they are all moved over to your other arm.

Purl Stitch

Purl stitch will be used with knit stitch in some patterns to create the look of different types of stitches. In arm knitting, to purl means to knit your stitches with the working yarn held to the back of your work, closer to you. If the pattern directs you to purl the first few stitches, the first stitch will be knitted as a knit stitch.

How to use purl stitch

First: Make a slipknot and cast on your stitches (see pages 20–23).

1. Hold the working yarn in the hand of the arm with the stitches on it.
2. Slip the first stitch off your arm and over the working yarn.
3. Holding the working yarn, turn the stitch toward yourself and slip it onto your other arm. Tighten the first stitch by pushing the "knot" up toward your arm while pulling the working yarn at the same time. All of your other stitches can be tightened by simply pulling on the working yarn.
4. Grab the working yarn from underneath your work with your right hand and hold it in the back of your work.
5. Slip the next stitch off of your right arm and over the working yarn.
6. This creates a purl stitch. Turn that stitch toward yourself and slip it onto your other arm.

Seed Stitch

The seed stitch is one of the more complicated arm knitting stitches. With this stitch you will be knitting your purl stitches and purling your knit stitches, creating the seed appearance as you would in needle knitting. In any pattern that uses the seed stitch, you will need to start your row with a knit and end your row with a purl. Every row will be as follows: Knit 1 stitch, purl 1 stitch. You need to have an even number of stitches to complete this stitch correctly. This causes you to knit your purls and purl your knits. This stitch is one of the "fuller" looking stitches and works best for projects where you want the stitches to be tighter.

How to use seed stitch

First: Make a slipknot and cast on your stitches (see pages 20–23).

1. Hold the working yarn in the hand of the arm with the stitches on it.
2. Slip the first stitch off your arm and over the working yarn.
3. While still holding the working yarn, turn the stitch toward yourself and slip it onto your other arm.
4. Tighten the first stitch by pushing the "knot" up toward your arm while pulling the working yarn at the same time. All of your other stitches can be tightened by simply pulling on the working yarn.

5. Move the working yarn from the front of your work to the back by picking up the skeins of yarn and moving them up and over your work to the back (closer to you).
6. Purl the next stitch by holding the working yarn to the back of your work as shown in photo 5 and pull the next stitch over and off your hand, just as you do when knitting a stitch.
7. Move the working yarn back to the front of your work (farther away from you) by picking up the skeins of yarn and moving them up and over your work, to the front.
8. Knit the next stitch.

Repeat these steps with all the stitches until they are all moved over to your other arm.

Tip

Seed stitch is a great stitch for creating throw rugs or similar projects where you want the piece to lay flat.

Linen Stitch

Linen stitch is also one of the fuller stitches. It is great for rugs, blankets, pillows, and other household accessories because this stitch lays flat—meaning the edges do not curl. With this stitch you will be knitting one stitch, moving the yarn to the back of the project as if to purl the next stitch, but you will slip the next stitch over to your other arm without purling it. Then you'll move the yarn back to the front and knit the next stitch. Be sure to cast on an even number of stitches and start with a knit and end with a slip. It is as if you are creating a "dash" when slipping the stitch and then moving the working yarn back to the front of your work. When knitting the linen stitch, you don't have to tighten the stitches dramatically, as it naturally tightens when making the "dash." If you tighten it too much it could make it difficult to move the stitches when you get a couple of rows into your project. Keep that in mind as you are arm knitting your rows.

How to use linen stitch

First: Make a slipknot and cast on your stitches (see pages 20–23).

1. Hold the working yarn in the hand of the arm with the stitches on it.
2. Slip the first stitch off your arm and over the working yarn.
3. While still holding the working yarn, turn the stitch toward yourself and slip it onto your other arm.
4. Tighten the first stitch by pushing the "knot" up toward your arm while pulling the working yarn at the same time. All of your other stitches can be tightened by simply pulling on the working yarn.
5. Move the working yarn to the back of the work.
6. Slip the next stitch over to your other arm.
7. Move the working yarn to the front of your work.
8. Knit the next stitch.

Repeat these steps with all the stitches until they are all moved over to your other arm.

Tip

Put your skeins of yarn in a bag—this makes it easy to move your yarn back and forth, and prevents the yarn from tangling.

Rib Stitch

Rib stitch adds depth and thickness to any project. This stitch looks best with the thickest, chunkiest yarns so that it stays full and you can see the different depths of the stitches. You can start with a knit or a purl and you can vary how many knits and purls you have in each row, as long as you knit your knit stitches and purl your purl stitches when switching from row to row. I prefer to start each row with purl stitches to prevent the edges from curling. Rib stitch is great for blankets because the more stitches there are the more you will be able to notice the difference in texture.

How to use rib stitch

First: Make a slipknot and cast on your stitches (see pages 20–23).

1. Hold the working yarn in the hand of the arm with the stitches on it.
2. Slip the first stitch off your arm and over the working yarn.
3. While still holding the working yarn, turn the stitch toward yourself and slip it onto your other arm.
4. Tighten the first stitch by pushing the "knot" up toward your arm while pulling the working yarn at the same time. All of your other stitches can be tightened by simply pulling on the working yarn.
5. Move the working yarn to the back of the work.
6. Purl the next purl stitches.
7. Move the working yarn to the front of your work.
8. Knit the next knit stitches.

Repeat these steps with all the stitches until they are all moved over to your other arm, then continue purling your purl stitches and knitting your knit stitches in every row.

Tip

I suggest Premier Yarns Couture Jazz or any giant-sized yarn for this stitch. You could also use three strands or more of super bulky yarn.

Cable Stitch

Cable stitch is beautiful for any project that will lay flat, such as a bag, blanket, or pillow. Choose a really chunky yarn for your project so that you are able to see the detail of this stitch. This stitch consists of purling the edges and knitting the stitches in the middle of the work. For example: Purl 3, knit 6, purl 3. You need to knit the same amount of purl stitches you have on each edge. You will slip the first half of the knit stitches off your arm and hold them to the back or in front of your project (as directed by your pattern) while you knit the next half of the knit stitches. Then you slip the first half of the knit stitches back onto the arm they came off and knit those same stitches.

How to use cable stitch

First: Make a slipknot and cast on your stitches (see pages 20–23).

1. Hold the working yarn in the hand of the arm with the stitches on it.
2. Slip the first stitch off your arm and over the working yarn.
3. While still holding the working yarn, turn the stitch toward yourself and slip it onto your other arm.
4. Tighten the first stitch by pushing the "knot" up toward your arm while pulling the working yarn at the same time. All of your other stitches can be tightened by simply pulling on the working yarn.
5. Keep the working yarn to the back of the work and purl the number of stitches indicated by the pattern.
6. Move the working yarn to the front of your work and knit the number of stitches indicated by the pattern.

Repeat those steps until you are ready to start the cable stitch.

7. Purl your purl stitches, then move the working yarn to the front of your work.
8. Slip half of your knits off your arm, place them on a pipe cleaner, and move them as directed by the pattern.
9. Knit the next half of your stitches.
10. Slip the knit stitches from the pipe cleaner back onto the arm you slipped them off and knit them.
11. Move the working yarn to the back and purl the remaining stitches.
12. Continue purling and knitting for the number of rows indicated by your pattern and then begin with the cable technique again.

Repeat these steps until your pattern is complete.

Tip

Use a pipe cleaner to slip the stitches off your wrist and hold them to the back or front of your work.

Garter Stitch

Garter stitch is so simple! With this stitch you will be moving the working yarn back and forth between rows, and that's it. It keeps the edges from curling so your pattern will lay flat, and adds texture and style to any project. Garter stitch takes two rows of knitting and then purling to see the results. I like to use this for straight scarves, some cowls, and even headbands to keep the edges flat.

How to use garter stitch

First: Make a slipknot and cast on your stitches (see pages 20–23).

1. Hold the working yarn in the hand of the arm with the stitches on it.
2. Slip the first stitch off your arm and over the working yarn.
3. While still holding the working yarn, turn the stitch toward yourself and slip it onto your other arm.
4. Tighten the first stitch by pushing the "knot" up toward your arm while pulling the working yarn at the same time. All of your other stitches can be tightened by simply pulling on the working yarn.
5. Knit all the stitches for one row.
6. Move the working yarn to the back.
7. Purl all stitches for one row.
8. Move the working yarn to the front of your work.

Repeat these steps for the entire pattern.

Tip

If you were to knit this stitch on needles, you would get the look of stockinette stitch, but because we are not turning our work between rows we get garter stitch with arm knitting.

Increasing Your Stitches

Increasing your stitches allows you to add stitches to a row to make your project wider at a certain point. This process works best when the first stitch of the row is a purl stitch so that you have a "knot" on the edge to pull the new stitch through. But it is not necessary since it will work well on any stitch. I like to use the increasing method when making headbands. You could also use it for boot cuffs, mug cozies, and similar items where you want to change the shape. It also works for projects which have smaller ends so you can add a button to one end to secure the item in place.

How to increase when arm knitting

First: Make a slipknot and cast on your stitches (see pages 20–23).

1. Hold the working yarn in the hand of the arm with the stitches on it.
2. Slip the first stitch off your arm and over the working yarn.
3. While still holding the working yarn, turn the stitch toward yourself and slip it onto your other arm.
4. Tighten the first stitch by pushing the "knot" up toward your arm while pulling the working yarn at the same time. All of your other stitches can be tightened by simply pulling on the working yarn.
5. Knit one row.
6. Move the working yarn to the back of the work.
7. Purl one row.
8. Increase one stitch by finding the knot of the first purl stitch on the end of your project on the previous row and pull that knot open.
9. Take the working yarn and put it under and through that knot, creating a new loop.
10. Slip this new loop onto the arm with all of the stitches on it. This creates a new stitch.
11. Knit this new stitch and all other stitches in that row.
12. Move the working yarn to the back of the work and purl the next row.

Repeat these steps as directed by the pattern.

Tip

Pay close attention to photos 8 and 9, where the loop is pulled through. Pulling it through the knot (pictured here) provides the most attractive results in the completed project.

Decreasing Your Stitches

Decreasing stitches allows you to eliminate stitches in a row to reduce the width of that row. This works very well for items that need to be round or triangular-shaped. You can decrease by knitting two stitches together at one time just as if they are one stitch. This can be repeated as many times as needed in one row, but it looks best when spread over multiple rows, decreasing by a couple of stitches in each row. I love to use the decreasing method for creating triangular shaped shawls and hats! It is such a simple way to create different shapes.

How to decrease when arm knitting

First: Make a slipknot and cast on your stitches (see pages 20–23).

1. Hold the working yarn in the hand of the arm with the stitches on it.
2. Slip the first stitch off your arm and over the working yarn.

3. While still holding the working yarn, turn the stitch toward yourself and slip it onto your other arm.
4. Tighten the first stitch by pushing the "knot" up toward your arm while pulling the working yarn at the same time. All of your other stitches can be tightened by simply pulling on the working yarn.
5. Knit your rows as directed by your pattern.
6. Decrease one stitch by knitting two stitches together as if they are one when directed by the pattern.
7. Continue knitting this row.

Repeat these steps as directed by the pattern.

Tip

The decreasing method works best when you arm knit with knit stitch.

Projects

Headband

That's right! You can knit an item as small as a headband with your arms. The best part is that it is completed in no time at all and costs very little. The headband gets the best results if made with two or three strands of super-bulky yarn. You can use a button to secure it in place or tie a knot using the leftover tail at each end. By decreasing and increasing your stitches, you will get a shape that will sit comfortably over your ears and on the back of your head.

Materials

1 skein of super-bulky yarn. 37 YD (34 m) is required for this project. I've used Premier Yarns Mega Tweed in White Tweed.

Measures approx:
L: 18 inches (46 cm)
W (at widest): 6 inches (15 cm)

How to make a headband

1. Pull 12 inches (30 cm) of yarn from the center of the skein and the outside of the skein and make a slipknot.
2. Using the two strands at the same time, cast on two stitches.
3. Row 1: Arm knit all stitches using knit stitch (see page 34).
4. Row 2: Move the yarn to the back, then purl all stitches.
5. Row 3: Increase by one stitch (see page 46), then knit the rest of the stitches.

→

Headband, continued

6. Row 4: Move the yarn to the back, then purl all stitches.

7. Row 5: Increase by one stitch, then knit all the stitches.

8. Row 6: Move the yarn to the back, then purl all stitches.

9. Row 7: Increase by one stitch, then knit all the stitches.

10. Row 8: Move the yarn to the back, then purl all stitches.

11. Row 9: Knit all stitches.

12. Row 10: Move the yarn to the back, then purl all stitches.

13. Row 11: Knit two, knit two together, then knit the rest of the stitches on that row.

14. Row 12: Move the yarn to the back, then purl all stitches.

15. Row 13: Knit all stitches.

16. Row 14: Move the yarn to the back, then purl one, purl two together, purl one.

17. Row 15: Knit two together, knit one.

18. Bind off one stitch, and knot the end.

19. Sew the ends of the headband together or add a large button to secure it in place when wearing it.

20. Weave in the ends and cut the yarn.

10-minute Beanie

10 mins

The 10-minute beanie can be worn by both men and women! If you would like to add some character, add a pom-pom to the top or a bow on one side. There are so many ways to dress up this hat. It is important to use a very bulky yarn or multiple bulky strands for this project or you will knit a hat with large holes. I recommend using one to two strands of a giant-sized yarn to get the best results.

Materials

1 skein of super-bulky yarn or 1 skein of giant yarn. 40 YD (38 m) is required for this project. I've used Red Heart Grande in Apricot.

Measures approx:
CIR: 20 inches (50 cm)
L: 9 inches (23 cm)

How to make a 10-minute beanie

1. Pull 2 feet (60 cm) of yarn from the center of the skein and make a slipknot.
2. Cast on 11 stitches.
3. Arm knit three rows using knit stitch (see page 34).
4. Row 4: Knit four, knit two together (see page 48), knit five.
5. Row 5: Knit all stitches.
6. Row 6: Knit three stitches, knit two together, knit two together, knit three.
7. Row 7: Knit all stitches.
8. Bind off.
9. Cut the excess yarn, leaving a 1½ foot (45 cm) tail.
10. Fold the hat in half. Pull the tail through all the stitches of the bind off edge and pull tight to cinch it.
11. Knot that end to keep it cinched tight.
12. Sew the sides together with the remaining tail and knot the end.
13. Weave in the ends and cut the yarn.

15 mins

Arm Muff

This arm muff is great paired with the headband (see page 52) since they both have matching stitches. You could coordinate them and use the same colored yarn. Use the thickest yarn possible for this project to avoid holes in your stitches. And remember to keep the stitches tight! This project is one of the easiest to arm knit, but everyone will be asking where you got such a great statement piece. Bring the arm muff back into style with this trendy way of knitting and a new style of yarn. Everyone will want one!

Materials

2 skeins of super-bulky or giant-sized yarn. 26 YD (24 m) is required for this project. I've used Premier Yarns Couture Jazz in Heliotrope.

Measures approx:
CIR: 14 inches (36 cm)
W: 11 inches (28 cm)

How to make an arm muff

1. Pull 2 feet (60 cm) of yarn from the center of the skein and make a slipknot.
2. Cast on eight stitches.
3. Arm knit six rows using garter stitch (see page 44). When you run out of yarn, tie a new skein to your yarn with a basic knot. Tighten the knot really well, pulling both ends firmly until the knot stops sliding. Cut the yarn ¼ inch (6 mm) from the knot.
4. Bind off the stitches and knot the end.
5. Sew on two extra-large buttons to secure it when wearing, as you would a sweater, or sew the ends of the arm muff together.
6. Weave in the ends and cut the yarn.

Boot Cuffs

Why not fake the look of the full boot warmer? It is so easy! You will add style to any pair of boots in a matter of minutes just by arm knitting a few rows of garter stitch. The boot cuffs sit at the top of the boots to give the illusion you're wearing full-length boot warmers. You can wear these with ankle, shin, or mid-calf boots. Adding buttons to the seam of each boot warmer will not only hide the seam, but also add some charm to this project. Choose a good super-bulky or giant yarn for this project.

Materials

1 skein of super-bulky yarn. 37 YD (34 m) is required for this project. I've used Premier Yarns Mega Tweed in White Tweed.

Measures approx:
L: 5 inches (12.5 cm)
W: 5 inches (12.5 cm)

How to make boot cuffs

1. Pull 12 inches (30 cm) of yarn from the center of the skein and the outside of the skein and make a slipknot.
2. Using the two strands at the same time, cast on four stitches.
3. Arm knit five rows using knit stitch.
4. Bind off the stitches and knot the end.
5. Sew the ends together (optional).
6. Add two medium size buttons to the seams of the cuffs. If you didn't sew them, use the buttons to secure them in place.
7. Weave in the ends and cut the yarn.

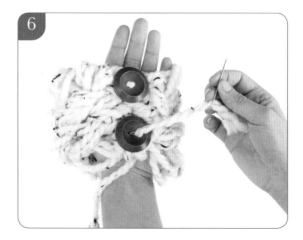

Chunky Cowl

This cowl is incredibly easy to make, but it looks so high fashion! This project is one of my most popular items. It can be completed in a matter of minutes and the yarn costs close to nothing. To keep the shape of this cowl, use the thickest yarn available. Use a yarn for this project that would be used on size 50 knitting needles or any giant-size yarn.

How to make a chunky cowl

1. Pull 1½ feet (45 cm) of yarn from the center of the skein and make a slipknot.
2. Cast on six stitches.
3. Arm knit 12 rows using knit stitch (see page 34). When you run out of yarn, tie a new skein to your yarn with a basic knot. Tighten the knot really well by pulling both ends firmly until the knot stops sliding. Cut the yarn ¼ inch (6 mm) from the knot.
4. Bind off the stitches and knot the end.
5. Sew the ends of the cowl together.
6. Weave in the ends and cut the yarn.

Materials

2 skeins of super-bulky or giant-sized yarn. 25 YD (23 m) is required for this project. I've used Premier Yarns Couture Jazz in Iron.

Measures approx:
CIR: 19 inches (48 cm)
W: 9 inches (23 cm)

Single Loop Infinity Scarf

This scarf is a lightweight accessory that drapes very comfortably. To add some character, make a miniature version of the headband or boot cuff (see pages 52 and 60) and wrap it around the finished scarf, securing it to one side with a large button. This scarf is one of my easiest and quickest arm knitting projects.

How to make a single loop infinity scarf

1. Pull 2 feet (60 cm) of yarn from the center of the skein and the outside of the skein and make a slipknot.
2. Using the two strands at the same time, cast on 10 stitches.
3. Arm knit 19 rows using knit stitch (see page 34).
4. Bind off the stitches and knot the end.
5. Sew the ends of the scarf together.
6. Weave in the ends and cut the yarn.

Materials

1 skein of super-bulky yarn. 120 YD (109 m) is required for this project. I've used Bernat Roving in Low Tide.

Measures approx:
CIR: 22 inches (56 cm)
W: 9 inches (23 cm)

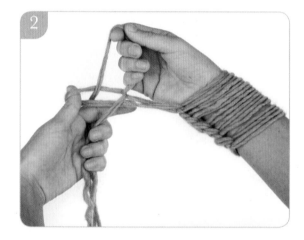

Tip

Pull a strand from the center and outside of the skein to avoid having to purchase two skeins for multiple strands.

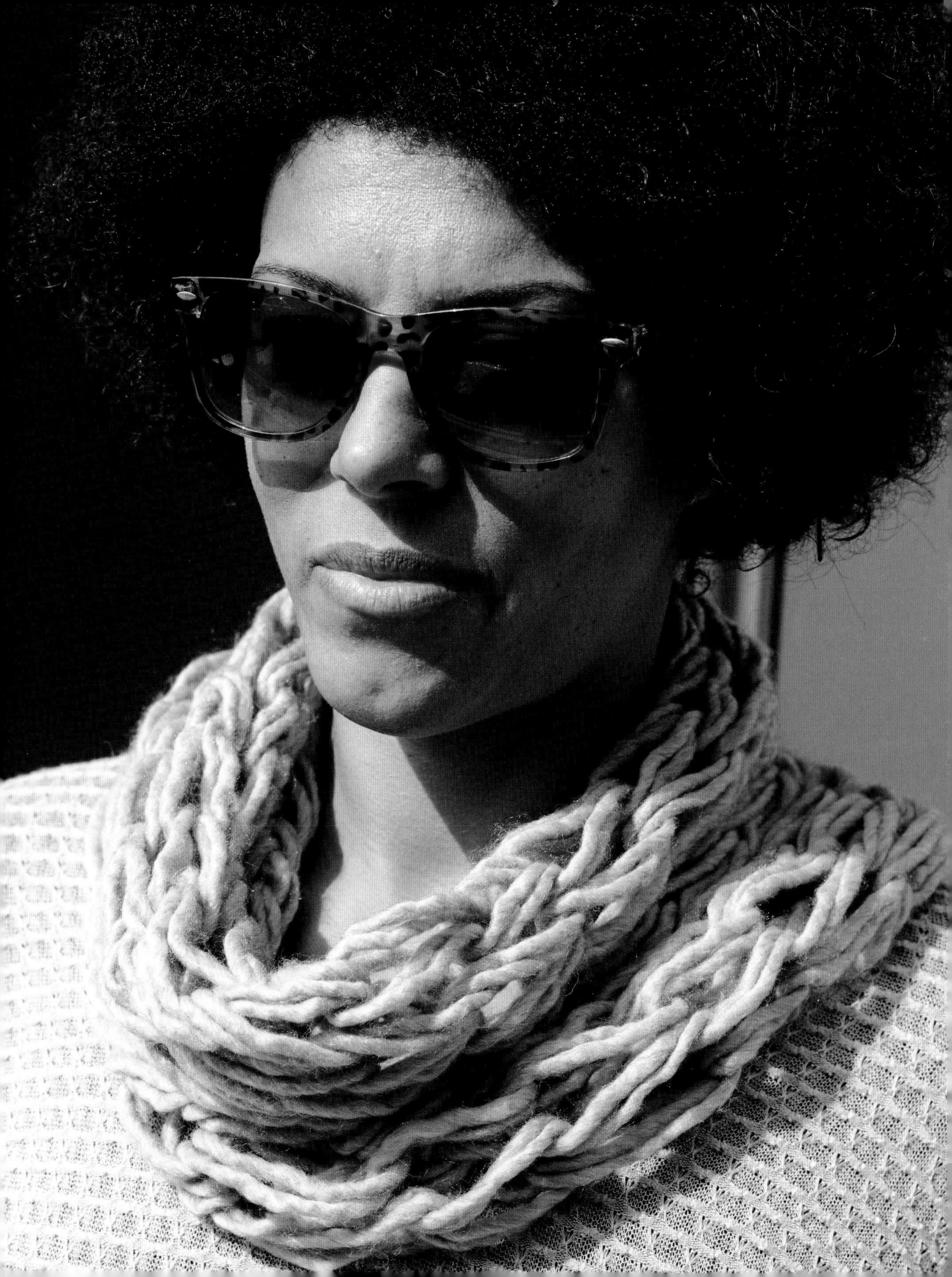

Baby Blanket

The best baby blankets are cozy, warm, and soft—
and that is exactly what you will get from this
pattern. The Couture Jazz yarn from Premier Yarns
works perfectly for this pattern. It is one of the
easiest and quickest patterns you will ever make.
The results are beautiful. Add stitches and rows
if you would like to make this blanket wider
and longer.

How to make a baby blanket

1. Pull 3 feet (90 cm) of yarn from the center of
    the skein and make a slipknot.
2. Cast on 11 stitches.
3. Arm knit 10 rows using knit stitch (see
    page 34). When you run out of yarn, tie a
    new skein to your yarn with a basic knot.
    Tighten the knot really well by pulling both
    ends firmly until the knot stops sliding. Cut
    the yarn ¼ inch (6 mm) from the knot.
4. Bind off the stitches and knot the end.
5. Weave in the ends and cut the yarn.

Materials

2 skeins of super-bulky
yarn. 33 YD (30 m) is
required for this project.
I've used Premier Yarns
Couture Jazz yarn
in Swan.

Measures approx:
L: 22 inches (56 cm)
W: 15 inches (38 cm)

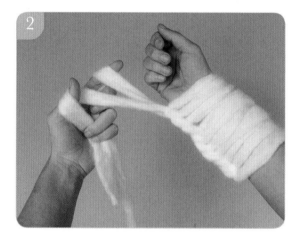

Super-fast Mug Cozy

Use this mug cozy around a coffee mug. You can even use it for cold drinks to keep your hands warm! When making the mug cozy, pull on each row once you are done knitting it to keep the project from bunching up. Using linen stitch with this project eliminates holes and keeps the stitches tight.

How to make a super-fast mug cozy

1. Pull 12 inches (30 cm) of yarn from the center of the skein and the outside of the skein and make a slipknot.
2. Using the two strands at the same time, cast on six stitches.
3. Arm knit five rows using linen stitch (see page 38).
4. Bind off the stitches and knot the end.
5. Sew the ends together.
6. Sew two buttons onto the seam with a darning needle (optional).
7. Weave in the ends and cut the yarn.

Materials

1 skein of super-bulky yarn. 45 YD (40 m) is required for this project. I've used Loops and Threads Cozy Wool in Goldenrod.

Measures approx:
CIR: 9 inches (23 cm)
W: 5 inches (12.5 cm)

Foot Stool Cover

This arm-knitted cover will add color and style to any round foot stool. You can even use it on a bar stool! This pattern will fit a stool with a seat diameter of approximately 14 inches (35 cm). To make a cover for a smaller stool, eliminate a row of arm knitting for every 2 inches (5 cm) smaller you would like it. For a larger stool, add a row of arm knitting for every 2 inches (5 cm) larger you would like it. There are two ways to finish this project. You can either sew the sides together before you place it on a stool, or you can place it on the stool then sew the sides together.

Materials

2 skeins of bulky to super-bulky yarn. 40 YD (37 m) is required for this project. I've used Premier Yarns Craft-Tee yarn in Light Green Shades.

Measures approx:
CIR: 44 inches (112 cm)

How to make a foot stool cover

1. Pull 4 feet (120 cm) of yarn from the outside of two skeins of Craft-Tee yarn and make a slipknot. (If you are using a different type of yarn, pull from the center, or the center and outside of one skein, as usual.)
2. Using the two strands at the same time, cast on 17 stitches.
3. Knit six rows using knit stitch (see page 34).
4. Row 7: Knit six, knit two stitches together, knit two stitches together, knit two stitches together, knit five.
5. Row 8: Knit all stitches.
6. Bind off the stitches and knot the end.
7. Pull the tail through all of the stitches on one end and pull tight to cinch the end. Make a knot to secure.
8. Use the same tail or the second tail to sew the two sides together. Place on the top of your foot stool and knot the end to secure.
9. Weave in the ends and cut the yarn.

Infinity Scarf

30 mins

This is the most popular arm knitting pattern in the world! It is so simple, but it looks amazing. This infinity scarf will never go out of style. It is your basic double-wrap scarf; to wear, hang it long as a single loop or wrap it twice around your neck. This is the first pattern I published on my blog back in 2011 and it made arm knitting go viral worldwide.

How to make an infinity scarf

1. Pull 2 feet (60 cm) of yarn from the center of the skein and the outside of the skein (or from the center of each skein if using two skeins of yarn) and make a slipknot.
2. Using the two strands at the same time, cast on eight stitches.
3. Arm knit 28 rows using knit stitch (see page 34).
4. Bind off and knot the end.
5. Sew the ends of the scarf together.
6. Weave in the ends and cut the yarn.

Materials

1 skein of super-bulky yarn. 90 YD (82 m) is required for this project. I've used Loops and Threads Cozy Wool in Sweet Grass.

Measures approx:
CIR: 48 inches (122 cm)
W: 6 inches (15 cm)

Cowl Scarf

This cowl is very warm and incredibly easy to make! Rib stitch will keep the edges from curling in and help the scarf keep its shape. Try to keep the stitches as tight as possible—that way the detail of the stitch will really stand out. The project requires two skeins of yarn to complete. However, you will be using three strands for knitting. For one skein, pull one strand from the center of the skein and another from the outside. For the other skein, pull the strand from the center, as usual. Using three strands will also help make the rib effect noticeable, even with the larger arm knit stitches. If you would like this scarf to fit a little more snugly, cast on six fewer stitches and adjust the rib stitch accordingly (see page 40).

How to make the cowl scarf

1. Pull 2 feet (60 cm) of yarn from the center of one skein, and from the center and outside of the other skein, and make a slipknot.
2. Using the three strands at the same time, cast on 18 stitches.
3. Arm knit 10 rows using rib stitch (see page 40), knit three, purl three, moving the yarn to the front of the work to knit and to the back of the work to purl.
4. Bind off and knot the end.
5. Sew the ends of the cowl together.
6. Weave in the ends and cut the yarn.

Materials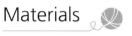

2 skeins of super-bulky yarn. 180 YD (164 m) is required for this project. I've used Loops and Threads Cozy Wool in Spearmint.

Measures approx:
CIR: 28 inches (71 cm)
W: 9 inches (23 cm)

Striped Cowl

The striped cowl sits comfortably and loosely from your collarbone to your chin. The stripes are simple to make, but they add such great character and style. You can also change the type of yarns you are using when you change color to add texture.

How to make a striped cowl

1. Pull 2 feet (60 cm) of yarn from the center and outside of the first skein and make a slipknot.
2. Using the two strands at the same time, cast on 10 stitches.
3. Arm knit three rows of your first color (here, the Grey Tweed) using knit stitch (see page 34).
4. Cut your first color 3 inches (7.5 cm) from your arm and tie on your second color (here, the Burgundy Tweed). Cut the excess.
5. Arm knit three rows of your second color using knit stitch.
6. Cut your second color 3 inches (7.5 cm) from your arm and tie on your first color again. Cut the excess.
7. Arm knit three rows of your first color using knit stitch.
8. Cut your first color 3 inches (7.5 cm) from your arm and tie on your second color again. Cut the excess.
9. Arm knit three rows of your second color using knit stitch.
10. Cut your second color 3 inches (7.5 cm) from your arm and tie on your first color again. Cut the excess.
11. Arm knit one row of your first color using knit stitch.
12. Bind off your stitches and knot the end.
13. Sew the ends of the cowl together.
14. Weave in the ends and cut the yarn.

Materials

2 skeins of super-bulky yarn in contrasting colors. 75 YD (68 m) is required for this project. I've used Premier Yarns Mega Tweed in Grey Tweed and Burgundy Tweed.

Measures approx:
CIR: 18 inches (46 cm)
W: 14 inches (36 cm)

Triplet Shawl

You can wear this shawl three ways: as an over-the-shoulder shawl; as a handkerchief-style scarf; or around your waist as a bikini cover-up. This shawl is so versatile you will be wearing it all year round. You can also select a light yarn, in a cotton and acrylic blend, rather than a warm, wool-blend yarn, such as the one I have suggested. For this project, you will make a basic triangle shape by decreasing your stitches (see page 48). You can add a fringe to this shawl too. Once you have completed step 7, weave both tails in and add a 5 inch (12 cm) fringe to both ends of the wider end of the shawl. Use the added fringe to tie a bow or knot to secure it around your shoulders or waist.

How to make a triplet shawl

1. Pull 2 feet (60 cm) of yarn from the center of one skein, and the center and outside of the other skein, and make a slipknot.
2. Using the three strands at the same time, cast on 28 stitches.
3. Row 1: Arm knit all stitches using knit stitch (see page 34).
4. Row 2: Arm knit two stitches together, arm knit to the last two stitches, then arm knit two stitches together (26 stitches remain).
5. Repeat Row 2 until there are four stitches remaining on your arm. You will have arm knit 13 rows altogether.
6. Row 14: Arm knit two together, arm knit two together.
7. Bind off the remaining two stitches and knot the end three times.
8. Weave in the ends and cut the yarn.

Materials

2 skeins of super-bulky yarn. 270 YD (246 m) is required for this project. I've used Loops and Threads Cozy Wool in Sea Storm.

Measures approx:
L: 53 inches (135 cm)
W (at widest): 16 inches (41 cm)

Knitted Bowl Cover

A knitted bowl cover adds a modern touch to a table or desk. You can keep anything in it—fruit, decorative items, even your yarn stash. It's a stretchy cover so fill it up! You can make this bowl cover match any room décor, just choose the color of the yarn to match or contrast with your room. If you want the bowl to be bigger, add a row of knit stitches for every 2 inches (5 cm) larger you would like it. Eliminate a row for every 2 inches (5 cm) smaller you would like it.

Materials

2 skeins of bulky to super-bulky yarn. 40 YD (37 m) is required for this project. I've used Premier Yarns Craft-Tee yarn in Peach Shades.

Measures approx:
CIR: 30 inches (76 cm)
D: 6 inches (15 cm)

How to make a knitted bowl cover

1. Pull 3 feet (90 cm) of yarn from the outside of two skeins of Craft-Tee yarn and make a slipknot. (If you are using a different type of yarn, pull from the center, or the center and outside of one skein, as usual.)
2. Using the two strands at the same time, cast on 14 stitches.
3. Arm knit five rows using knit stitch (see page 34).
4. Row 6: Knit five, knit two stitches together, knit two stitches together, knit five.
5. Bind off the stitches and knot the end.
6. Pull the tail through all of the stitches on one end and pull tight to cinch the end. Make a knot to secure.
7. Use the same tail or the second tail to sew the two sides together. Place on your bowl and knot the end to secure.
8. Weave in the ends and cut the yarn.

Mega Infinity Scarf

This project is similar to the infinity scarf (see page 72), but quite a bit chunkier. This scarf will, no doubt, be one of the warmest you will ever wear. Use three strands of yarn at one time to achieve the super-chunky effect, and a wool-blend yarn for durability. This scarf will never go out of style.

How to make a mega infinity scarf

1. Pull 3 feet (90 cm) of yarn from the center of each of the three skeins and make a slipknot.
2. Using the three strands at the same time, cast on 11 stitches.
3. Arm knit 30 rows using knit stitch (see page 34).
4. Bind off the stitches and knot the end.
5. Sew the ends of the scarf together.
6. Weave in the ends and cut the yarn.

Materials

3 skeins of super-bulky yarn. 318 YD (291 m) is required for this project. I've used Lion Brand Wool-Ease Thick and Quick in Raspberry.

Measures approx:
CIR: 34 inches (86 cm)
W: 14 Inches (36 cm)

Tip

Use three skeins at one time, pulling a strand from the center of each skein. If you want to make the scarf a bit longer and you run out of yarn, tie a new skein to your yarn with a basic knot. Tighten the knot really well, pulling both ends firmly until the knot stops sliding. Cut the yarn ¼ inch (6 mm) from the knot.

Basic Shawl

It is best to use a couple of strands of super-bulky yarn for this basic shawl to keep it looking full. Garter stitch will also help this beautiful shawl keep its shape. You can wear this item as a shawl or as a bikini cover-up—the pattern will make a rectangular shape that will drape nicely over your shoulders or hips. If you intend to wear it as a summer shawl, opt for a cotton-blend yarn to keep it light. Sew a large button on one corner to secure it when wearing, or simply tie a loose knot using two of the corners.

Materials

2 skeins of super-bulky yarn. 180 YD (164 m) is required for this project. I've used Loops and Threads Cozy Wool in Merlot.

Measures approx:
L: 42 inches (107 cm)
W: 17 inches (43 cm)

How to make the basic shawl

1. Pull 3 feet (1 m) of yarn from the center of each of the skeins and make a slipknot.
2. Using the two strands at the same time, cast on 13 stitches.
3. Arm knit 30 rows using garter stitch (see page 44).
4. Bind off and knot the end.
5. Weave in the ends and cut the yarn or use them to secure the ends together with a knot.

Cable Blanket

This is a very light and fluffy blanket. Arm knitting with cable stitch adds depth and texture, making it cushiony and comfortable. This may look like a complicated project, but once you get the hang of it you will fly through the pattern. Remember to have a pipe cleaner nearby to slip the stitches onto—hold them at the front or back of your work as directed.

Materials

8 skeins of bulky to super-bulky yarn. 104 YD (95 m) is required for this project. I've used Premier Yarns Couture Jazz Sparkle in Fresh Snow Sparkle.

Measures approx:
W: 24 inches (60 cm)
L: 38 inches (96 cm)

How to make a cable blanket

1. Pull 4 feet (120 cm) of yarn from the center of the skein and make a slipknot.
2. Cast on 16 stitches.
3. Row 1: Purl four stitches, knit eight stitches, purl four stitches, moving the yarn to the front of the work to knit and to the back of the work to purl.
4. Repeat Row 1 for the next three rows.
5. Row 5: Purl four, slip four stitches onto a pipe cleaner and hold them in the front of your work, knit four, slip those four stitches back onto the same arm, knit four, purl four.
6. Row 6: Purl four, knit eight, purl four.

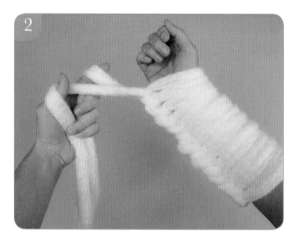

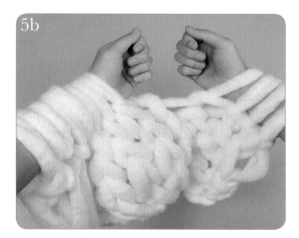

Cable Blanket, continued

7. Repeat Row 6 for the next two rows.

8. Row 9: Purl four, slip four stitches and hold them to the front of your work, knit four, slip those four stitches back onto the same arm, knit four, purl four.

9. Row 10: Purl four, knit eight, purl four.

10. Repeat Row 10 for the next two rows.

11. Row 13: Purl four, slip four stitches and hold them at the back of your work, knit four, slip those four stitches back onto the same arm, knit four, purl four.

12. Row 14: Purl four, knit eight, purl four.

13. Repeat Row 14 for the next two rows.

14. Row 17: Purl four, slip four stitches and hold them at the back of your work, knit four, slip those four stitches back onto the same arm, knit four, purl four.

15. Row 18: Purl four, knit eight, purl four.

16. Repeat Row 18 for the next two rows.

17. Row 21: Purl four, slip four stitches and hold them at the back of your work, knit four, slip those four stitches back onto the same arm, knit four, purl four.

18. Row 22: Purl four, knit eight, purl four.

19. Repeat Row 22 for the next two rows (24 rows in total).

20. Bind off and knot the end.

21. Weave in the ends and cut the yarn.

Cloud Cowl

Cloud cowls are made to be lightweight, simple, and easy to throw on with any outfit. The combination of the soft, roving yarn and the perfect fit to keep your neck and chin warm will make you never want to take this cowl off when there is a chill in the air. Seed stitch (see page 36), while a little more time consuming, keeps the cowl light and airy while adding an interesting, unique design.

Materials

2 skeins of super-bulky yarn. 90 YD (82 m) is required for this project. I've used Loops and Threads Cozy Wool in Harvest.

Measures approx:
CIR: 16 inches (40 cm)
W: 14 inches (36 cm)

How to make a cloud cowl

1. Pull 2 feet (60 cm) of yarn from the centers of the two skeins and make a slipknot.
2. Using the two strands at the same time, cast on 12 stitches.
3. Arm knit 10 rows using seed stitch, knit one, purl one throughout every row, moving the skeins of yarn to the front and back of your cowl as you knit.
4. Bind off and knot the end.
5. Sew the ends of the cowl together.
6. Weave in the ends and cut the yarn.

Tip

This project takes slightly longer than the other scarves featured in this book because you are arm knitting with seed stitch. The extra effort for the detail in the stitch is worth it, though!

Circular Mat

This circular mat looks great in front of a vanity, by your nightstand, or even as a centerpiece mat on your dining table. Be creative! Choose a durable yarn for this project. If you want a larger mat or an area rug, just keep knitting the rows until you have the desired width when it is arranged as a circle.

How to make a circular mat

1. Pull 12 inches (30 cm) of yarn from the outside of two skeins of Craft-Tee yarn and make a slipknot. (If you are using a different type of yarn, pull from the center, or the center and outside of one skein, as usual.)
2. Using the two strands at the same time, cast on two stitches.
3. Arm knit 110 rows using knit stitch (see page 34).
4. Bind off one stitch and knot the end.
5. On a flat surface, begin spiraling the long strand of knit stitches upside down so the wrong side of the work is facing up. Arrange the work in a circle.
6. Take a long piece of yarn and weave it through the stitches that are sitting side by side. Connect them all to secure the circle in place.
7. Knot the end.
8. Weave in the ends and cut the yarn.

Materials

2 skeins of super-bulky yarn. 80 YD (73 m) is required for this project. I've used Premier Yarns Craft-Tee yarn in Light Green Shades.

Measures approx:
CIR: 45 inches (114 cm)

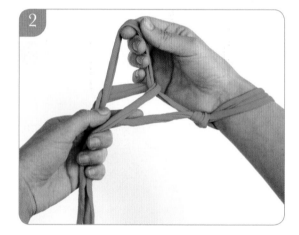

Basic Blanket

This will most likely be one of the coziest blankets you will ever have. You will want one for every room of your home. It adds a modern, yet homely style when displayed. To get the best results, choose the bulkiest yarn you can find for this project. Knit stitch is the simplest of the arm knitting stitches so your blanket will be complete in no time at all!

How to make a basic blanket

1. Pull 5 feet (150 cm) of yarn from the center of one skein and make a slipknot.
2. Cast on 17 stitches.
3. Arm knit for 28 rows using knit stitch (see page 34).
4. When you run out of yarn, tie a new skein to your yarn with a basic knot. Tighten the knot really well by pulling both ends firmly until the knot stops sliding. Cut the yarn ¼ inch (6 mm) from the knot.
5. Bind off your stitches and knot the end.
6. Weave in the ends and cut the yarn.

Materials

8 skeins of bulky to super-bulky yarn. 132 YD (120 m) is required for this project. I've used Premier Yarns Couture Jazz in Iron.

Measures approx:
L: 45 inches (114 cm)
W: 34 inches (86 cm)

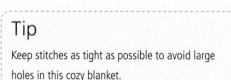

Tip

Keep stitches as tight as possible to avoid large holes in this cozy blanket.

Shopper Bag

This bag is a great statement piece to take with you to a farmer's market or even to the beach! Linen stitch is ideal for this project because it is a tighter stitch, leaving only small holes in your work. For this project, the directions call for working with three strands of yarn. You can also use just two strands, as in the photo (right). For two strands, you will need one less skein of yarn.

How to make a shopper bag

1. Pull 3 feet (90 cm) of yarn from the centers of three of the skeins and make a slipknot.
2. Using the three strands at the same time, cast on 14 stitches.
3. Arm knit 20 rows using linen stitch (see page 38).
4. Bind off the stitches and knot the end.
5. Fold the bag in half inside out and sew the sides together, using the tails if possible.
6. Weave in the ends and cut the yarn.

How to make the strap

7. Using two strands at the same time, cast on two stitches.
8. Arm knit 12 rows using knit stitch (see page 34). Pull on the end to stretch the strap.
9. Bind off one stitch and knot the end.
10. Cut the yarn long enough to tie the strap on the inside edge of the shopper bag where it is not visible. Secure it with a double knot and repeat for the other end of the strap.
11. Cut the excess yarn.

Materials

4 skeins of bulky to super-bulky yarn. 172 YD (78 m) is required for this project. I've used Premier Yarns Macra-Made in Cayenne Pepper.

Measures approx:
L: 17 inches (43 cm)
W: 7 inches (18 cm)
Strap: 26 inches (66 cm)

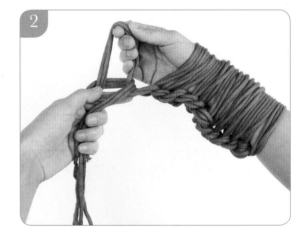

Chunky Rug

This rug is very durable—I use it as a place to put my shoes by my front door. You could even use this as a decorative placemat for pet dishes. Be creative with this project and use it in a variety of ways! This pattern creates a basic rectangular shape, about 21 by 17½ inches (53 by 44 cm), and uses the beautiful linen stitch so it lays flat.

How to make a chunky rug

1. Pull 4 feet (120 cm) of yarn from the centers of two of the skeins and make a slipknot.
2. Using the two strands at the same time, cast on 18 stitches.
3. Arm knit 20 rows using linen stitch (see page 38). When you run out of yarn, tie a new skein to your yarn with a basic knot. Tighten the knot really well by pulling both ends firmly until the knot stops sliding. Cut the yarn ¼ inch (6 mm) from the knot.
4. Bind off the stitches and knot the end.
5. Weave in the ends and cut the yarn.

Materials

3 skeins of bulky to super-bulky yarn. 129 YD (117 m) is required for this project. I've used Premier Yarns Macra-Made yarn in Butter.

Measures approx:
L: 21 inches (53 cm)
W: 17½ inches (44 cm)

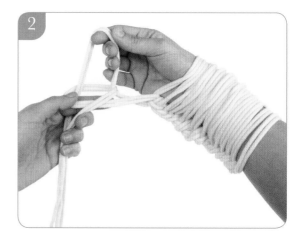

Tip

Choose a yarn that is machine washable for this project. Retain the yarn wrapper—it will always have instructions for care.

Winter Snood

You can wear this snood as a chunky cowl or place it over your head for extra warmth. It is great for cold, windy weather if worn as a scarf. Using two strands at one time with a super-bulky yarn will keep the snood warm, thick, and luscious. If you would like the scarf to be secured when wearing it as a snood, simply sew a large button where it would sit just above your collarbone. Using the Mega Tweed yarn from Premier yarns allows this project to drape comfortably so you can wear it in different ways.

Materials

2 skeins of super-bulky yarn. 148 YD (136 m) is required for this project. I've used Premier Yarns Mega Tweed in Burgundy.

Measures approx:
CIR: 24 inches (60 cm)
W: 22 inches (56 cm)

How to make a winter snood

1. Pull 3 feet (90 cm) of yarn from the centers of both of the skeins and make a slipknot.
2. Using two strands at one time, cast on 16 stitches.
3. Arm knit 14 rows using knit stitch (see page 34).
4. Bind off the stitches and knot the end.
5. Sew the ends of the winter snood together.
6. Weave in the ends and cut the yarn.

Straight Scarf with a Fringe

Stay warm and cozy with this bulky textured scarf. This type of scarf has been around forever and now you can knit it so much faster with arm knitting! Although I have recommended a particular type of yarn, you can use any fiber blend with this scarf, as long as it has the proper thickness. It can also be tied many different ways because of the length—you'll never get tired of wearing it. Even though you will be taking an extra step by adding a fringe to this scarf, you can still complete it in under an hour.

Materials

2 skeins of super-bulky yarn. 148 YD (136 m) is required for this project. I've used Premier Yarns Mega Tweed in White Tweed.

Measures approx:
L: 68 inches (173 cm)
W: 9 inches (23 cm)

How to make a straight scarf with a fringe

1. Pull 2 feet (60 cm) of yarn from the centers of each of the skeins and make a slipknot.
2. Using the two strands at the same time, cast on eight stitches.
3. Arm knit four rows using garter stitch (see page 44).
4. Knit 25 rows using knit stitch (see page 34)
5. Knit four rows using garter stitch.
6. Bind off the stitches and knot the end.
7. Weave in the ends and cut the yarn.
8. Cut approximately 32 strands of yarn, 8 inches (20 cm) each in length.
9. Fold two strands in half. Insert the fold into the first stitch on the end of your scarf.
10. Insert your index finger and thumb into the fold and grab the ends of the fringe. Pull it through to knot and secure the fringe.
11. Repeat steps 9 and 10 until you have attached the fringe on both ends of your scarf.

Pet Bed

What pet would not want a bed made out of cozy wool? This pet bed made with cable stitch, is designed so that you can insert a cushion or pillow in the center before sewing up the last side. You can also use it without an insert as I did with my pet bed. This project is perfect for a small dog or a cat. To make a larger pet bed, follow the pattern for the cable blanket instead (see page 86). When you get to step 15 of that pattern, continue knitting the rest of the rows. When you have completed the arm knitting, fold the blanket in half and follow this pattern from step 16.

Materials

5 skeins of super-bulky yarn. 65 YD (60 m) is required for this project. I've used Premier Yarns Couture Jazz Sparkle in Pumpkin Pie Sparkle.

Measures approx:
L: 17 inches (43 cm)
W:15 inches (38 cm)

How to make a pet bed

1. Pull 4 feet (120 cm) of yarn from the center of the skein and make a slipknot.
2. Cast on 12 stitches.
3. Row 1: Purl three stitches, move the working yarn to the front of your work, knit six stitches, move the yarn to the back of your work, purl three stitches.
4. Repeat Row 1 for the next two rows.
5. Row 4: Purl three, slip three stitches onto a pipe cleaner and hold them at the back of your work, knit three, slip those three stitches back onto the same arm, knit three, purl three.
6. Row 5: Purl three, knit six, purl three.
7. Repeat Row 5 for the next three rows.
8. Row 9: Purl three, slip three stitches and hold them in front of your work, knit three, slip those three stitches back onto the same arm, knit three, purl three.

Pet Bed, continued

9. Row 10: Purl three, knit three, purl three.

10. Repeat Row 10 for the next three rows.

11. Row 14: Purl three, slip three stitches and hold them at the back of your work, knit three, slip those three stitches back onto the same arm, knit three, purl three.

12. Row 15: Purl three, knit six, purl three.

13. Row 16: Knit all stitches.

14. Repeat Row 16 for the next four rows (total of 20 rows).

15. Bind off and knot the end.

16. Fold the bed in half and use the same or a similar color yarn to sew all three sides together with a darning needle. If you like, insert stuffing or a pillow before sewing the last side.

17. Weave in the ends and cut the yarn.

Chunky Rug with a Fringe

This rug is cozy and feels fantastic underfoot. It would look great beside your bed, on the floor in front of a sink, or anywhere you would like to add a little extra comfort. This pattern creates a basic rectangular shape, about 22 by 17½ inches (56 by 44 cm). To make this pattern even easier, reduce the number of rows by half and skip the part where you fold the rug in half and sew the edges together. The rug will not be as full and comfortable but will still look great and will add color and style wherever it is placed.

Materials

2 skeins of bulky to super-bulky yarn. 180 YD (164 m) is required for this project. I've used Loops and Threads Cozy Wool in Goldenrod.

Measures approx:
L: 22 inches (56 cm)
W: 17½ inches (44 cm)

How to make a chunky rug with a fringe

1. Pull 5 feet (150 cm) of yarn from the centers of the two skeins and make a slipknot.
2. Using the two strands at the same time, cast on 30 stitches.
3. Row 1: Knit three stitches, move the working yarn to the back of your work, purl three stitches. Repeat knit three, purl three, moving your yarn as you go, until you come to the end of the row.
4. Row 2: Purl three stitches, move the working yarn to the front of your work, knit three stitches. Repeat with purl three, knit three, moving your yarn as you go, until you come to the end of the row.

→

Chunky Rug with a Fringe, continued

5. Repeat steps 3 and 4 until you have arm knitted a total of 12 rows.
6. Bind off your stitches and knot the end.
7. Fold the rug in half and sew the three edges together.
8. Weave in the ends and cut the yarn.
9. Cut approximately 40 pieces of yarn, 7 inches (18 cm) each in length.
10. To make the fringe, using one piece of yarn at a time, fold your first piece of yarn in half. Find the first stitch on the end of the rug, insert your index finger and thumb in the stitch, and grab the fold of the fringe. Pull it through the stitch approximately 1 inch (3 cm) and pull the ends of the fringe through that 1 inch (3 cm) loop. Tighten to secure.
11. Continue adding the fringe along both ends of the rug.

Cross Body Bag

The cross body bag is a modern take on a string bag—great for carrying larger items. This bag can be held comfortably across the body. Using cable stitch on the front side of the bag but knit stitch on the back helps it to be practical. The strap is simple to make, using just three strands of yarn and tying a basic knot to secure it in place. For this project, the directions call for working with two strands of yarn. But for a fuller look, feel free to use three strands, as in the photo (right). For three strands, you will need one more skein of yarn.

Materials

2 skeins of bulky to super-bulky yarn. 86 YD (78 m) is required for this project. I've used Premier Yarns Macra-Made in Papaya.

Measures approx:
W: 21 inches (53 cm)
H: 9 inches (23 cm)
Strap: 31 inches (79 cm)

How to make a cross body bag

1. Pull 3 feet (90 cm) of yarn from the center of the skeins and make a slipknot.
2. Using two strands at the same time, cast on 12 stitches.
3. Row 1: Purl three stitches, move the yarn to the front of your work, knit six stitches, move the yarn to the back of your work, purl three stitches.
4. Repeat Row 1 for the next two rows.
5. Row 4: Purl three stitches, slip three stitches onto a pipe cleaner and hold them to the front of your work, knit three stitches, slip those three stitches back onto the same arm, knit three, purl three stitches.
6. Row 5: Purl three stitches, move the yarn to the front of your work, knit six stitches, move the yarn to the back of your work, purl three stitches.

→

Cross Body Bag, continued

7. Row 6: Purl three stitches, move the yarn to the front of your work, slip three stitches and hold them at the back of your work, knit three stitches, slip those three stitches back onto the same arm and knit them. Move the working yarn to the back of your work, purl three stitches.

8. Row 7: Purl three stitches, slip three stitches and hold them at the back of your work, knit three stitches, slip those three stitches back onto the same arm and knit them, purl three stitches.

9. Arm knit for five rows using knit stitch.

10. Bind off your stitches.

11. Fold the bag in half inside out and sew the sides together using the tails if possible.

12. Weave in the ends and cut the yarn.

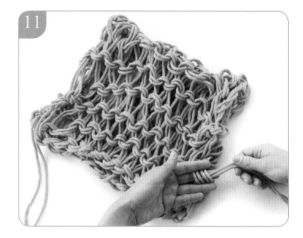

How to make the strap

13. Cut three strands, approximately 4 feet (120 cm) each in length.

14. Tie the strap on the inside edge of the cross body bag where it's not visible. Secure it with a double knot and repeat with the other end of the strap.

Basic Straight Scarf

The basic straight scarf is a great unisex accessory. There are many different ways to wear this scarf. You can wrap it once, tie it in a knot, make a loop and pull the ends through . . . the possibilities are endless. Using rib stitch will prevent the edges from curling in and help the scarf lay flat.

Materials

2 skeins of bulky to super-bulky yarn. 148 YD (136 m) is required for this project. I've used Premier Yarns Mega Tweed in Burgundy Tweed.

Measures approx:
L: 70 inches (178 cm)
W: 4½ inches (11.5 cm)

How to make a basic straight scarf

1. Pull 2 feet (60 cm) of yarn from the center of each of the two skeins and make a slipknot.
2. Using two strands at the same time, cast on six stitches.
3. Arm knit 40 rows using rib stitch (see page 40), knit two, purl two, knit two, moving the yarn to the front of the work to knit and to the back of the work to purl.
4. Bind off the stitches and knot the end.
5. Weave in the ends and cut the yarn.

Decorative Throw

The decorative throw is a great lap blanket for any chilly day. The color and texture of this blanket will add an inviting touch to any room in your home. If you would like to make this blanket larger, cast on four extra stitches and adjust the knit two, purl two stitches accordingly. This will require approximately three more skeins.

Materials

6 skeins of bulky to super-bulky yarn. 78 YD (72 m) per skein. I've used Premier Yarns Couture Jazz Sparkle in Amber Waves.

Measures approx:
L: 39 inches (99 cm)
W: 23 inches (58 cm)

How to make a decorative throw

1. Pull 4½ feet (135 cm) of yarn from the center of the skein and make a slipknot.
2. Cast on 14 stitches.
3. Arm knit 22 rows using rib stitch (see page 40), knit two, purl two, moving the yarn to the front of the work to knit and to the back of the work to purl.
4. When you run out of yarn, tie a new skein to your yarn with a basic knot. Tighten the knot really well by pulling both ends tightly until the knot stops sliding. Cut the yarn ¼ inch (6 mm) from the knot.
5. Bind off your stitches and knot the end.
6. Weave in the ends and cut the yarn.

Throw Pillow

This throw pillow is the perfect size to use on a couch, chair, or bed. Since you are knitting with linen stitch, there are not very many holes in the stitches. This means you have the option of stuffing it with polyester fiberfill, or you can buy a pillow that fits inside. If you would like to make the pillow smaller, eliminate five rows from the pattern. This will make a more rectangular-shaped throw pillow.

How to make a throw pillow

1. Pull 4 feet (120 cm) of yarn from the centers of both skeins and make a slipknot.
2. Using the two strands at the same time, cast on 20 stitches.
3. Arm knit 40 rows using linen stitch (see page 38).
4. Bind off the stitches and knot the end.
5. Fold the pillow in half, turn it inside out, and sew the sides together.
6. Stuff the pillow with polyester fiberfill or insert a pillow.
7. Sew the last edge.
8. Weave in the ends and cut the yarn.

Materials

2 skeins of super-bulky yarn. 212 YD (194 m) is required for this project. I've used Lion Brand Wool-Ease Thick and Quick yarn in Spice.

Fiberfill or a pillow insert

Measures approx:
L:17 inches (43 cm)
W:17 inches (43 cm)

Resources

Reading Yarn Labels

It is important to understand the information that is provided on yarn labels and to be able to decode the symbols on them. There is no standardized label system, and information can vary considerably between yarn manufacturers. However, most labels provide the general information listed below.

Yarn weight

A yarn weight is usually provided to offer information on the use of a yarn. A name of weight may be given, such as "lace" for very fine yarns; "DK" for medium-weight yarns; and "Bulky," "Super-Bulky," or "Chunky" for heavier yarns. The best results when arm knitting, of course, come from using the heaviest yarns.

Alternatively, a ply is given. This is a number ranging from the finest to the heaviest yarn weights (usually between 1 ply and 20 ply). Another system is also used, generally in the US, of numbering yarn weights from 0 to 7, where 0 is the finest yarn and 7 the heaviest.

See page 14 for more information about yarn weight.

Fiber content

A yarn's fiber content is usually supplied on the label. For example: 80 percent bamboo, 20 percent wool. This relates to the fibers that make up the yarn, as often one yarn can feature several different fiber sources. This information is important to know when it comes to caring for your yarn.

Yardage and weight

The wrapper will tell you the total length of yarn in a skein. This will help you work out how much you will need for a certain knitting project, whether the yarn is good value for money; and suggests the yarn weight (whether it is Fine, Medium, or Bulky).

Color number and dye lot

Dye lots are important if you require multiple skeins of yarn of the same color for your knitting project. Always buy yarn from the same dye lot, as dye lots do vary in color, and even a subtle variation may show up in the final piece.

Care instructions

Care instructions provide vital information on how to wash and dry a knitted garment. The main care symbols are listed in the table on the next page.

Basic Shawl (see page 84 for pattern)

Yarn Wrappers

Some of the information provided on yarn wrappers, such as tension and needle size, is specific to needle knitting. As you knit without needles and control the tension yourself when arm knitting, the weight and fiber is of more importance when deciding on your yarn. It is useful to keep the yarn wrapper for the care instructions, though!

Care instructions

Handwash in lukewarm water

Handwash in warm water

Do not machine- or handwash

Three variations of the machine-washable symbols. A delicate cycle is advisable for all handknitted items; set the machine cycle to match the wash temperature.

Drying instructions

Lay flat to dry
Sometimes this symbol appears under the washing symbols

Machine dryable
If a temperature is indicated, follow that recommendation

Do not machine dry

Bleaching

Chlorine bleaching okay
Always test bleach on a sample swatch of the yarn

Do not use bleach

Ironing Instructions

Press with a cool iron

Press with a warm iron

Press with a hot iron

Do not iron

Dry-cleaning instructions

Do not dry-clean

Can be dry-cleaned with all solutions

Can be dry-cleaned only with fluorocarbon or petroleum-based solutions

Can be dry-cleaned only with perchlorethylene, fluorocarbon, or petroleum-based solutions

Shopper Bag (see page 96 for pattern)

Yarn Substitutions

There are several reasons why you may want to substitute a yarn. On page 130 are some general guidelines to assist you in your decision-making process. Each arm knitting project in this book includes the information that you need to substitute the yarn (equivalent to the yarn gauge in needle knitting) and each project states how many skeins are required, and further details as to how many yards or meters of yarn are necessary to complete the project in full in one sitting.

Reasons you might need to, or want to, substitute yarn:

- The suggested yarn is too expensive for your budget, or you want to test a pattern with a cheaper yarn choice before you arm knit with the real thing.

- You don't like the color choices in the suggested yarn range and would prefer another.

- You are allergic or sensitive to a suggested yarn, and would prefer a more hypo-allergenic choice.

- The suggested yarn may not be readily available or may have been discontinued.

- You may prefer a different feel and surface texture to the suggested yarn.

- You may have chosen a particular yarn first because you fell love with it, and are looking for a suitable arm knitting pattern for it.

Winter Snood (see page 100 for pattern)

Yarn Substitutions, continued

Drape and elasticity

Drape and elasticity are crucial elements to consider when substituting yarn. If you would like to match the look of a knitted project in this book, stick closely to the drape and elasticity specifications of the suggested yarn. For example, if you substitute cotton for wool, the finished garment may drop and sag excessively because cotton is less elastic than wool; conversely, using wool instead of cotton may shrink or distort the fit of the finished garment.

Fiber content

Fiber content will affect the performance and overall look of the knitted pattern. Look at the information supplied on the yarn's character to judge its suitability as a substitute yarn. For example, acrylic mixed with nylon is a good substitute for wool, as the nylon adds enough elasticity to match that of wool.

Yardage

Calculate the yardage for a substitute yarn by checking the total yarn requirements of the item you wish to knit. For example, if the suggested requirement for the pattern is 10 multiplied by 50 g skeins, each with a yardage of 92 YD, the total yardage is 9,200. If the substitute yarn offers 110 YD per 50 g skein, divide the total yardage by the yardage of a single skein to obtain the number of skeins required overall: 9,200 YD divided by 110 YD = $8^{3}/_{10}$ skeins. Of course, you always need to round up, so in this example you would need to buy 9 skeins.

Care instructions and wearability

The care instructions of a yarn will affect the end result of the knitted garment in terms of its drape, softness, shrinkage, and performance. Many fibers change with wearing and washing; some soften, increasing their drape more, some pill, and some shrink. If any of these factors are the reason why you want to substitute the suggested yarn, refer to the specific yarn information for consideration.

Circular Mat (see page 92 for pattern)

Calculating Yardage & Weight

Calculating yardage is not an exact science, but there is a simple method you can use to get you in the ballpark and nail down a more accurate guesstimate.

How to calculate

1. Arm knit a swatch with the yarn you want to use for your pattern in the garment's main stitch and measure the width and height.
2. Unravel the swatch (snip off any long ends) and measure the length of yarn.
3. Multiply the swatch width and height to calculate the total square inches/centimeters.
4. Divide the total square inches/centimeters by the amount of yarn you used.

For example, I knitted a swatch 4 inches (10 cm) square. When I unraveled the yarn it was $17\frac{3}{4}$ YD (16.2 m). I multiplied the measurements of my swatch to estimate the coverage area of the garment, then divided this by the amount of yarn I'd used. My swatch measured 4 × 4 inches and I used $17\frac{3}{4}$ YD of yarn for this. To work out how much yarn I needed per square inch, I calculated as shown in equation A.

These instructions are especially useful if you want to move on to arm knitting garments. You then need to calculate the overall area of the fabric used, as follows.

1. Block-sketch your pattern using a rectangle.
2. Take the longest and widest measurements that you calculated during your "deconstruct to reconstruct" phase and apply them to your blocks. Remember, this is going to be a rough guide and it's best to have some yarn left over.

3. Multiply the length and width of each block and add them all up to get the total area of your garment in square inches (don't forget to double them if you only drew one block for one side).
4. Multiply the total square inches by the yarn length per square inch to give the total amount of yarn required (equation B).
5. Don't forget to add in extra for details such as straps. When in doubt, always round up.

If the yarn I want to use comes in 221-YD skeins, I would divide the total amount of yarn required by the skein length as shown in equation C.

Add 20 percent to cover any unforeseen inaccuracies. In the above example, I'd buy seven skeins of yarn for my pattern.

A.
16 [size of swatch] ÷ $17\frac{3}{4}$ [yarn used] = 0.91 YD

B.
1,386 [total square inches] × 0.91 [YD per square inch]
  = 1,261 [total amount of yarn YD required]

C.
1,261 [garment coverage in square inches]
  ÷ 221 YD [skein length] = $5\frac{3}{4}$ skeins

Cloud Cowl (see page 90 for pattern)

US/UK Glossary

American and European knitting terms and measurements sometimes differ; this can be confusing when following instructions or yarn requirements from a knitting pattern or reading information from a yarn wrapper. The following tables will assist in converting information.

Conversion Formulas

To convert inches to centimeters, multiply by 2.54; to convert centimeters to inches, multiply by 0.394.
To convert yards to meters, multiply by 0.914; to convert meters to yards, multiply by 1.094.
To convert ounces to grams, multiply by 28.35; to convert grams to ounces, multiply by 0.035.

Measurement Conversions	
Imperial	Metric
$\frac{1}{8}$ in	3 mm
$\frac{3}{8}$ in	1 cm
1 in	2.54 cm
12 in (1 ft)	30 cm
1 yd	91.44 cm
1 yd 3 in	1 m

Weight Conversions	
Imperial	Metric
1 oz	28 g
1 lb (16 oz)	450 g
2 lb 3 oz	1 kg (1,000 g)

Yarn and measurement information on this page and page 14 sourced from ravelry.com and the Craft Yarn Council.

Basic Blanket (see page 94 for pattern)

Glossary of Terms

Abrasion resistance
The ability of a fiber, yarn, or knitted structure to be scratch- or itch-free against the skin.

Arm knit
To knit a pattern using your arms as the needles.

Artisan
Handspun or hand-tailored yarns, usually made in limited editions, small productions, or one-off batches.

Bind off
To end the arm knitting part of the project. This creates a clean edge.

Bulky yarn
Also referred to as chunky yarn, it is a 12–16 ply yarn. This is normally used on size 5.5–8 mm knitting needles and is generally the best choice for arm knitting projects.

Cast on
To create new stitches using the tail of yarn and working yarn. This is done at the beginning of every arm knitting project.

Chunky knitting weight
A heavy or thick knitted structure in a fabric. Also referred to as "bulky" yarn weight: a heavy or thick yarn.

CIR
An abbreviation indicating circumference.

Craft yarn
A heavy yarn weight, or a thick yarn.

Decreasing
Arm knitting two stitches together, as if those two stitches are one stitch.

Drape
The ease and flow of movement in a garment. The softer the flow of a knitted fabric, the more drape it has; the sturdier the fabric, the less drape it has.

Durability
The long-lasting performance of a knitted fabric.

Fiber
A natural or synthetic filament that may be spun into a yarn.

Giant yarn
The largest size of yarn available. This is normally used on size 50 (25 mm) knitting needles.

Hypoallergenic yarn
Yarn designed to minimize the possibility of an allergic response, as the material contains relatively few or no potentially-irritating substances.

Increasing
Pulling the working yarn through the first purl stitch on the edge of your project to create a new stitch. This will make one more stitch on your arm.

Knit a stitch
The working yarn will be in the front of your work (farther from you). Arm knit the stitches with the working yarn in the front.

Move the working yarn to the back
Pick up the skein of yarn and move it up and over your work to the back. This allows you to purl stitches.

Move the working yarn to the front
Pick up the skein of yarn and move it up and over your work to the front. This allows you to knit stitches.

Nap
The fuzzy, downy coating of the surface of a knitted fabric or yarn.

Glossary of Terms, continued

Ply
The twisting together of two or more strands.

Purl a stitch
The working yarn will be at the back of your work (closer to you). Arm knit the stitches with the working yarn at the back.

Roving
A single-ply yarn that is loosely twisted and felted as a thick yarn.

Rug
A heavy yarn weight, or a thick yarn.

Sew the ends or sew the sides
Wrapping or weaving a strand of yarn through two ends or two sides of an arm knitted project.

Shrinkage
The calculated decreasing in size of a knitted stitch or fabric post-knitting and post-washing.

Skein
Yarn, wound into a long coil, rather than a ball shape.

Slipknot
The first step for any arm knitting project and also the first stitch. It is a knot created with two ends of the yarn. It can tighten and loosen easily for different-sized arms.

Snags
Knitted stitches that are pulled or caught accidently from the knitted structure, causing large unsightly loops.

Stitch
Makes up the body of work.

Stitch definition
The clarity or visibility of a knitted stitch.

Super-bulky yarn
A 16 or more ply yarn, normally used on size 10 mm or larger knitting needles.

Surface texture
The visual and tactile quality of a knitted fabric.

Tail of yarn
The second strand of yarn used to cast on your stitches. Also known as "tail." It is the end you don't work with.

Tension
The firmness or looseness with which one arm knits.

Variegated
A yarn with various colors in it.

Weave in the ends
Pull the excess tail of yarn left over at the end of your project through the sewn edge, the cast on edge, or the bind off edge. This will guarantee a secure, finished edge to any arm knit project.

Working yarn
The yarn being pulled from the center of the skein. This is what you use to create the rows of arm knitting.

Yardage
The number of yards or meters in a skein of yarn. It is used to help determine how much yarn one requires for a knitted item, or the weight of a yarn.

Arm Muff (see page 58 for pattern)

Useful Websites

For more useful tips, and if you have any arm knitting questions, go to my website: **www.simplymaggie.com**

YARN MANUFACTURERS

www.premieryarns.com

For specialty yarns, such as Couture Jazz yarn, Couture Jazz Sparkle yarn, Craft-Tee yarn, Macra-Made yarn, and Mega Tweed yarn.

www.craftsy.com

For basic bulky and super-bulky yarn.

www.michaels.com

For basic bulky and super-bulky yarns, such as Loops and Threads Cozy Wool yarn, and Lion Brand Wool-Ease Thick and Quick yarn.

www.woolwarehouse.co.uk

For basic chunky or super-chunky yarns.

www.deramores.com

For basic chunky or super-chunky yarns.

KNITTING TIPS

There are a vast number of online forums that supply knitting tips, helpful hints, and knitting patterns, from independent knitters to chat forums and yarn companies. It is not possible to supply an exhaustive list, so I chose the following based on clarity of information and a good choice of knitting techniques—both arm knitting and needle knitting.

dailyknitter.com

A lovely-looking website with patterns, knitting help, book and yarn reviews, and a directory of knitting sites and forums.

patonsyarns.com.au

A site with an illustrated guide to knitting techniques. Also supplies free downloadable knitting patterns.

lanagrossa.com

Offers free downloadable knitting tips and techniques, including specialist techniques such as "binding off Italian style" and "fringing."

KNITTING ASSOCIATIONS

craftyarncouncil.com

A knitting association website representing yarn companies, accessory manufacturers, magazine and book publishers, and consultants in the yarn industry. This is a valuable resource for knitters of all levels. It supplies a calendar of knitting events and expos, and links to guilds and groups.

tkga.com

The Knitting Guild Association is a membership-based nonprofit organisation, and its website has links to books, magazines, groups, and events.

YARN SUPPLY AND YARN INFORMATION

There is a daunting choice of online knitting-supply stores. However, there are very few stores that present information beautifully, with easy-to-read websites, and that also have good, reliable customer service. I list a few recommended sites below.

knit.net.au

A beautifully designed website from a manufacturer that supplies its own range of yarn and patterns. It also provides information on the welfare of the sheep from which it sources its yarns.

loveknitting.com

An online store supplying a wide range of yarns sourced from around the globe. Allows you to search by yarn weight, fiber type, and yarn brand. Also has a category for eco-friendly fibers. Provides good descriptions of each yarn, with suggested knitting uses.

knitpicks.com

An online yarn supplier with a diverse range of globally sourced yarns, as well as knitting kits, tools, and patterns. This site also has tutorials for all knitting levels, and links to online knitting community forums.

Basic Straight Scarf (see page 116 for pattern)

Index

Acknowledgments

A special thank you to Premier Yarns *www. premieryarns.com* for providing many of their yarns for the projects in this book.

I also want to thank Peter Weber of Peter M. Weber Photography for being such a pleasure to work with while he photographed all of the step-by-step photos and swatches for the book.

Thank you to RotoVision, of course, for reaching out to me to be the author of this book. I am most certainly an arm knitting enthusiast and it has been a great experience being able to share my patterns and ideas with all the other crafters.